THOUGHT PROCESS

It All Starts With A THOUGHT

PULKIT HASIJA

Wordsbrew
An imprint of BlueRose Publishers

Title: THOUGHT PROCESS
Language: ENGLISH
Character set encoding: UTF-8

First published by

Wordsbrew
An imprint of BlueRose Publishers

An Imprint of BlueRose Publishers

Head Office: 123, First Floor,
Ansal Bhawan, 16, K.G. Marg,
Connaught Place, New Delhi - 110001
+91-8882 898 898

Wordsbrew
An imprint of BlueRose Publishers

Dedication

This book is dedicated as a gift to my parents. Somehow it is for the reason that, I have written this book. Somewhere on purpose or unintentionally they have motivated, in fact provoked me to write. In that sense, they are also the co-authors of this book. Thought Process is about how different brains functions in a different way. It is about understanding that a thought if executed properly can become a business, a thought if interpreted and conveyed properly, it can cherish relationships and lives. However if a thought is interpreted in a wrong way, or if it is a negative thought it can ruin relations, it can makes us feel depressed and unconventional. Through this book I am trying to demonstrate the impact of thoughts we get and the impact of one's thought process (the way we think). How our thoughts influences our lives. The purpose of this book is to enhance the way we contemplate.

ACKNOWLEDGEMENTS

No matter how much efforts we human beings put in, whatever that Almighty God has planned, will definitely going to happen. It is my first book and prior to this I have never ever imagined that one day I may become an author. Perhaps that was a call of that Almighty Lord. I would like to bow down to him and thank him for manifesting this writing edict for me. I would also like to acknowledge my parents for provoking me to take a step forward to do something which I never thought to do even in my dreams. i.e. writing a book. I have been in nexus with Sister B.K. Shivani and Sadguru. I follow both of them on YouTube. I would also like to thank them. Through their seminars and videos I was able to accomplish some confidence and they certainly helped me in completion of my book.

FOREWORD

How the book came to fruition?

Human beings have a fickle mind which can make the immovable ambiance move all over this universe in a fraction of seconds. It is our duty to control this fickle mind. Whatever we see, hear, observe around ourselves, our brain gets those messages and once brain gets any message it starts decoding those messages. Then we start getting various thoughts knocking at our brain.
This book came to fruition when I realized that a single thought can have different impact on two different individuals and how it can convert a normal conversation to an argument or a conflict, this is because of the different approach and different thought process of two different individuals. A single thought can develop oxidation in relations.

I took a lot of efforts in writing this book. Prior starting and during my writing I kept on observing the behavior of strangers, my relatives, friends and of all those whom were in contact with me. While writing, I also recalled some memories of mine, my friends, my relatives and my neighbors. Those memories have moreover helped me in reciting some of the experiences which were experienced for the reason that of double edged sword thinking. I also did some online and offline research. I interviewed some random layman individuals to get the flavor.

How to read this book and get the best out of it?

It is a nonfiction book. Each and every chapter in this book can be read in isolation. There is no sequence which is to be charted in reading this book; however it is advisable to start it from beginning and proceed ahead. It is a motivational book so whichever chapter you read, you will get the gist of it. I have also factored in some exercises for our readers, through which they can gauge themselves and moreover analyze where and how they can improve. The phrases, sentences or words which lights up a fire in you and motivates you kindly highlight them or make a note of those.

Why I chose to put down this book and why the theme is THOUGHT PROCESS?

All thoughts do not become things, but all things were thought. PRIOR EXISTENCE THIS BOOK WAS ALSO A THOUGHT.

I thought to write, that is why this book exists. When I thought to write, I thought on which theme shall I write? Through this thought, I thought to write on THOUGHT PROCESS.

To accomplish any milestone one has to start his/her journey. It is said that those who fail to plan, plan to fail. Moreover, the first principal of management is planning. And to plan, first we have to analyze opportunity, identify the aim, explore the options, select best option, and then implement the best. For all the above activities, be it analyzing, identifying, exploring we have to put our thinking cap on and have to do some brain storming. That is why THOUGHT PROCESS plays a very vital role in achieving greatness irrespective of what your field is.

Subsequently it is our THOUGHT PROCESS or our THINKING that either manipulates us or provides us the right direction.

There is a saying that,"Winners don't do different things, they do things differently."

Ever wondered how they do things in a diverse manner, how they add value to every task they do. Their approach and attitude is different from others. There are ordinary people and there are extraordinary people. The extraordinary ones are those who go an extra mile each time, putting in much more effort than looked-for. There is just an extra they do under the sun, that is why they are extraordinary and differ from ordinary. Now the question comes up what makes them to walk an extra mile?

The answer to the above question is: THOUGHT PROCESS. It is their thought process that motivates them to think out of the box. That is why they take a leap in the dark, come at something new, strain to innovate, and leave no stone unturned to bring a change in a traditional way of doing things.

PREFACE

During the entire process of writing this book and even when the book was completed, I was thinking and wishing this book to be a masterpiece and a huge success.

I THOUGHT that this book will be appreciated by my readers when it will be released, however it does not matters what I, being an author thinks and wish for this book; what readers think about my book will make it or break it. The readers THOUGHT PROCESS will prevail over the writer's THOUGHT PROCESS. Here also thinking has come into play.

The author has written it with a Thought Process of

- making it a best seller,
- being this book on the crest of the wave,
- and coming up with the flying colors.

However, there is a possibility that you; being a reader may not like it contrary to my expectations; being an author. Your Thought Process about this book will decide this book's future.

Similarly in life, THOUGHT PROCESS plays a very significant role and sometimes it's not our THOUGHT PROCESS which impacts us, its the THOUGHT PROCESS of other individuals as well whom we perceive as our friends, well wishers, relatives or even strangers.

PROLOGUE

About the Author

In spite of being a normal and healthy person, I was taken to The Neurologist for medical examination. Not only to Neurologist, moreover I was also being engaged for a Psychiatrist appointment by my mother for my checkup. My parents were worried about me for the reason that they observed unexpected and drastic changes in my behavior and attitude. These behavioral changes were for the reasons that some thoughts which struck in my mind. My thought process was somehow different comparatively to others. Such THOUGHT PROCESS of mine made me felt like stupefied every time. It was my altogether a different THOUGHT PROCESS which didn't gain me appreciation however I earned a lot of criticism.

I was born and brought up in Gurugram in a small midst class family. I was an intelligent and a good student from my childhood time. My relatives had developed a thought process about me and a perception that I will achieve something immense one day. However many a time, I tend to forget things. Due to this Forgetfulness, I kept on losing my confidence, as I continuously encountered failures in every venture of my life. I enrolled for professional courses and failed many times. Joined lots of jobs and was never satisfied with my jobs and felt like my jobs are full of envy. Since my childhood time I had a passion for doing my own business, however being born in a poor family, due to lack of funds and absence of parents got behind for business, I joined service industry. I have worked with BPO, Banking, Insurance Underwriting, Mutual Fund, Telecom, Retail and Accounting sector. However was never satisfied with jobs as my THOUGHT PROCESS was provoking me that I should do my own business. Due to this thought, somehow I took my jobs for granted and failed in every job I did. Got terminated from jobs, due to bad performance in corporate. I was put into performance improvement plans. I tried Financial Planning business and failed, tried cafe business and failed, tried online business and failed, played chess at nationals and International open level and failed there also. I lost all of my money in options and stock market which I pulled in from my jobs. I borrowed money from bank and lost that money and left with no source of income. I landed myself between a rock and a hard place. Received a lot of criticism and almost lost my identity and existence. Still I did not lost my courage for learning something new, I did not lost my courage for starting my own business, courage to do what I want. It was my THOUGHT PROCESS that let me hold on to my nerves.

EPIGRAPH

- I think Ronald Reagan was one of the great presidents, period, not just recently. I thought he had the demeanor. I thought he had the bearing. I thought he had the thought process. **Donald Trump**

- A lot of times when people are released or, unfortunately, get fired, they almost scramble for what it is they are going to do next. I think when you are no longer working under a big, corporate umbrella; you have to be your own brand, your own enterprise. That was my thought process before I left. **Cody Rhodes**

- When you look at a movie, you look at a director's thought process. **Oliver Stone**

- Film-making is not a one man show. It is not like I am thinking something and they are expressing it. I try to pull the actor in and together we try to get the expression. It is not my thinking alone, it is our thinking. The actor also becomes a part of the thought process. **Mani Ratnam**

- Education is the best way to relieve someone from a bad thought process. **Bret Bielema**

- I cannot teach anybody anything; I can only make them think. **Socrates**

- We are what we think. **Buddha**

- There is nothing on earth that you cannot have once you have mentally accepted the fact that you can have it. **Robert Collier**

CONTENTS

1. MOST WONDERFUL BLESSED WITH MOST WONDERFUL

God has brought forth this universe. God thought to create, this conception (the creation of whole universe) was once a thought in God's mind. The almighty has bent lots of creatures such as insects, birds, animals, mountains, rivers. However human being is the most wonderful creation of God. It is for the reason that we human beings are blessed with a wonderful organ i.e. brain and a wonderful skill i.e. a unique THOUGHT PROCESS. Thinking is uncomfortable, it demands effort and only human can make efforts while thinking analytically, critically and logically. That is why Human beings deserve to have a meaningful life which is full of wealth, prosperity, happiness, health and joy.

Human being's life is different from the life of birds, animals, insects and other creatures. It is because of this brain and we can think the other way round. Their brain may be bigger however ours brain is better, because we can give ourselves extra cortex to do more things than just to operate our body. We are not just stick to fulfill our basic needs of food, shelter and clothing. We want to makes our life safe, comfortable (luxurious) with almost zero exposure to struggle. That is why we human keep on inventing something new, day in and day out enhancing our standard of living. Wonderful scientific inventions which have made our life relaxed, they were also a thought in the mind of those scientist who made that thought a reality. Being a human is like to keep learning and improvising new things. Unlike animals and birds we can plan our future. We can make provisions for future emergencies and contingencies. We can think for others, for society however on the other hand, other creature's thoughts are limited to quench their hunger and thirst only.

We are blessed with the most imposing intelligence. It is because human beings have brain which can be utilized to make this earth a paradise. However, on the other hand being a human can be considered as a curse.

BEING HUMAN IS A CURSE: Thinking capability has enabled humans to be the most successful, creative and destructive beings on the planet. We have an amazing capacity to craft, innovate, and show compassion and care. It can sadly go wrong. We indulge our brain in becoming superior; we consider ourselves the most precious species and this belief tend us to pass over the nature. We have turned ourselves into a white elephant (costlier however useless). We cut forests, we kill birds and animals. We destroy nature. This world needs love to hold out and human beings were designed to spread love and happiness. However to thrive for success and power we have turned a destroyer from a survivor. We are spreading diseases, we are creating pollution, and we are creating a imbalance in nature.

Since we all are blinded by power and the thought that we are the ultimate and best creation of GOD. So this thought of being the best creature has developed an endless pride and cruelty in us, which comprises of a lot of negative consequences. These consequences can be comparison with other species and within humans itself. If there is a comparison then there is an inference such as who is better among ourselves. Then we twitch to come along with the competition, feelings of hate and jealousy. Slowly and gradually we humans have develops an intoxication of our own power, wealth and superiority. While trying to prove the best we human beings also do away with animals, birds, forests and even harm our own human race.

All such consequences crop up for the reason that we think we are the ones who deserve under the sun at any cost. We are living in such an environment in which some people use to flaunt their false pride.

Let me brief you a scenario: A few days back I heard a man talking on cellphone and saying that he has been prosecuted for a half murder case and this man was like being proud while saying so. I pity on such people and their thoughts. The person who thinks that he deserves applaud due to such violent activity, we cannot imagine his future actions derived from his THOUGHT PROCESS. They can be the future criminals or terrorists. No doubt thoughts play a vital role in developing our attitude and our future.

On the other hand

BEING HUMAN IS A BENEDICTION: We as a human being have unimaginable powers through which we can achieve spiritualism, we can make for towards society. There is a set of capabilities that we human have that transcends anything else that exists. Being a human being is a sacred sign because not only we have the capability to study ourselves we can study others as well, be it a living or a non-living compound. The human brain is also seems special in the amount of energy that it uses. We as a human being have the power to control the planet because we are the only animals that can co-operate both flexibly and in very large numbers. We can do multitasking unlike other insects, animals or birds. We can invent things that can prove to be a boon for current and forthcoming generations. That is why being a human is a blessing. Apart from thinking function our brain is designed to discriminate between the good and the evil. As we have the power to differentiate between good and bad we also have the power to implement what is good and to avoid what is bad. That is why we can put in at every aspect positively, provided we use our brain and our thoughts wisely. Being a human is to cram, understanding the causes and effects.
Being a Human Being can be a sacred sign as well as can be a curse. It depends on our thought process, how we want to take it forward.

All day long we have ideas that could change lives, which

could change the world. When we woke up in the morning our brain starts working. It is operational till we sleep and moreover it also works while we sleep; in our dreams. Our brain has something to play with every now and then. It never rests. Our lifestyle, surroundings, aims and aspirations bring forth our thoughts. However, we can change our thoughts according to our will.

Watch your thoughts; they become words. Watch your words; they become actions. Watch your actions; they become habits. Watch your habits; they become character. Watch your character; it becomes your destiny. Lao-Tze

Our mind cannot hold back thinking and imagining. From the moment we wake till the time we die, our minds are constantly churning through thoughts. Most of these are everyday thoughts to get through the day such as what to have for breakfast or what clothes to wear. Some are more life-changing such as who to ask out, or what career options to pursue. Our mind is like a baby who plays with a toy (thought). It needs a toy. Thoughts are like toys for our mind. Thoughts can be arrived in our mind through various modes. Such as normal communication, receiving any criticism or a compliment, any called for or order received. These all things give birth to thoughts in our mind. If we get a thought in our mind, it is like a cold day in July to cut that thought then and there. To forget that thought or to cut it we have to get another thought. Our mind and thoughts can keep ourselves distracted, and we may become absent minded most of the time. When we are work we fantasize about our vacations and when we are at vacations we starts worrying about the work piling at our desk. The law of substitution says," Your mind can hold only one thought (positive or negative) at a time. Any thought which enables us to take action, if it is being repeated it becomes a habit. Hence if some positive actions are being taken on a repeated basis it develops a positive attitude and a positive thought process. According to the law of belief," Whatever we believe with conviction; becomes our reality?"

As I have brought up earlier that mind is like a baby who needs a toy to play with. Let's say if a baby breakdown for a big toy and we offer him a small one he will not hold back breaking down. However if we offer him that big toy he will let up crying. Similar is the case is with human brain. If we feel like that a particular thought is not good or it is unpleasant or like a fish out of water, then we have to change the thought.

LET'S DO AN EXERCISE:

For each question there are five options, choose the option that best answers the query according to you. Each option consists of a certain weight age. Note down your answers on a paper and at the end of the quiz for each option score card is given; add up all the points as per your responses.

Question: What do you dislike the most about yourself?

Option A: You ask people for help once in a blue moon

Option B: You don't stick up for yourself

Option C: You are impatient and little insecure

Option D: You doubt everything in life

Option E: You take too many risks

Question: What is most important to you right now?

Option A: Your Goals

Option B: Your Family

Option C: You Friends

Option D: Your Job or Career

Option E: You Yourself

Question: A black cat crosses your path, you think?

Option A: I wonder where it's going

Option B: I will be alright

Option C: It's all superstitious

Option D: I am cursed

Option E: I will keep an eye forward for someone else to walk past

Question: Pick a word to describe your life

Option A: Confusing

Option B: Blessed

Option C: Crazy

Option D: Lonely

Option E: Unpredictable

Question: What is your idea about bad day

Option A: Disagreement with someone

Option B: Life is too short to have a bad day

Option C: Sickness

Option D: Every day that I wake up

Option E: Internet down everywhere

Question: Wake up in morning with a feeling

Option A: Alert and ready

Option B: Peaceful and happy

Option C: Rested enough

Option D: Going back to sleep again

Option E: Too tired, sluggish

Question: What makes you laugh?

Option A: Witty jokes

Option B: Everything

Option C: Sarcasm

Option D: Random internet meme

Option E: Clumsy people

Question: What is your favorite color?

Option A: White, black, red

Option B: Bright color Rainbow

Option C: Yellow, blue, green

Option D: Color? You are racist

Option E: Other colors or I don't know

Question: Quote that best suits you

Option A: I don't know where I am going but I am on my way

Option B: The best is yet to come

Option C: The best way out is always through

Option D: All good things come with a price

Option E: If opportunity doesn't knock, build

Question: A word to describe your life

Option A: Confusing

Option B: Blessed

Option C: Crazy

Option D: Lonely

Option E: Unpredictable

Time to reveal the results:

Option A=50 Points, Option B= 40 Points, Option C= 30 Points, Option D= 20 Points and Option E= 10 Points.

If your score is between 100-160 points, you are an opportunist for whom the world is a place full of many opportunities and possibilities. You are flexible and see the world in a different prospective.

If your score is between 170-250 points, you are often viewed as a negative person, however reality is a bit differ. You are skeptic who needs proof

If your score is between 260-350 points, you are realistic and optimistic who see the things as they are. You are independent and practical minded and you don't sugarcoat the things.

If your score is between 360-440 points, you are a contented and cheerful person who nine times out of ten keeps an eye at the brighter side, the world for you is full of sunshine and you appreciate little things in life. Highly Optimistic

If your score is between 450-500 points you have a bright outlook on the future. You keep an eye around for things that hold deeper significance and strife to form genuine relationships. Helping others brings joy to you.

The above assessment is the purpose to check how you see, analyze and think. It also demonstrates the quality of your analyzing and thinking.

Thought Process Cycle:

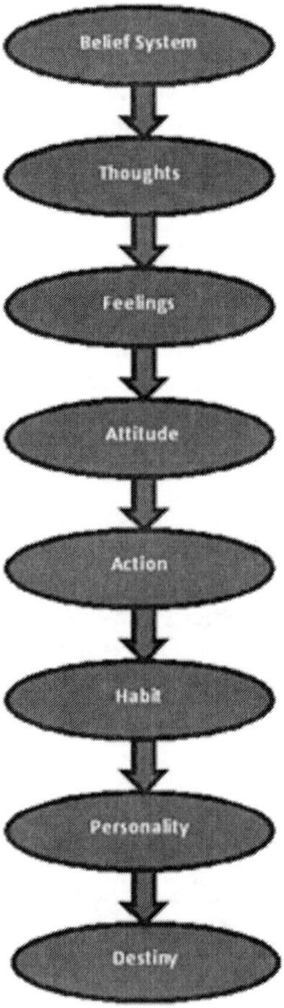

Belief system of everyone is different. It is dependent on the information we are receiving, the past experience we had.

The belief system serves as a raw material. As two different individuals had a different raw material, hence the finished product will also be diverse. The belief system is intangible and is not visible however the finished product is visible. The finished product of belief system will be how you treat someone, your behavior, and attitude. Whatever is being fed in our mind, our body will react accordingly. Once it becomes your behavior your actions will be according to behavior, which becomes the habit. This habit comes along the personality which determines your destiny. Feelings and emotions are merely our body's reaction to our mind's action. So forth we think our body reacts accordingly. Both of these are distinctive, however complexly related and have a profound impact.

Ever pondered how a great business has become such great, because someone behind that business had an idea up their sleeve. The idea for any business is generated by thinking and analyzing the current problems and finding a solution to it. Today's successful business person had thought of an opportunity or an idea in their initial stages. It is that thought only that has given a birth to a business. These successful people have a diverse mindset and thought process. They come at to find opportunity in every problem they face. Unlike other individual who gets stuck, these people think out of the box because of:
The approach they have in their thinking and analyzing. That is why THOUGHT PROCESS is a crucial element that makes human beings unique.

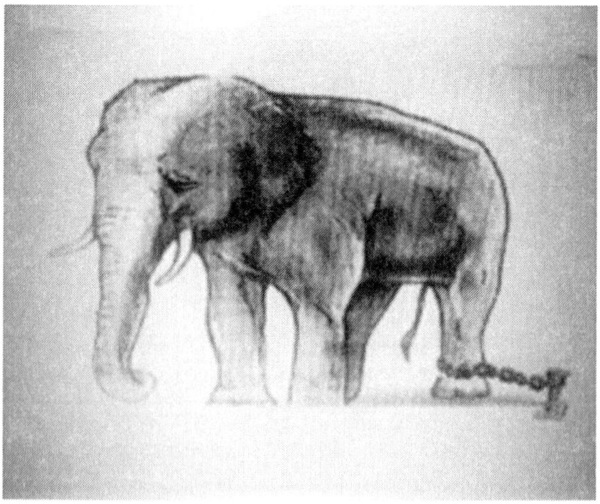

While beholding at the above picture, did you recall something? There is a story about a man who used to pass by from a way daily. He daily sees an elephant, whose leg has been tied with a small rope along a peg. It seemed that the elephant could have easily broken away that rope with a small effort. Out of curiosity that man asked elephant's trainer the reason if that elephant has ever tried to get away by breaking that rope? The trainer replied that when the elephant was very young and much smaller, he was tied with that very rope. At that time it was enough to hold him here. As the elephant grew up he couldn't even realize his potential for the reason that his belief system and past experience has made him believe that he still cannot get away. Thoughts crafts emotions, and that initial thought in the mind of elephant has already brought forth an emotion that he is too week to halt that rope and get away from it. This practice is usually used by circus administrators to keep a circus elephant from running away.

One thought jolts an endless chain of other thoughts.

A single sight, a small whisper, a rumor, a loud noise, a knock at the door is enough for our mind to start diving in the immense ocean of thoughts. And when we start swimming in the ocean of our thoughts our mind starts doing lots of programming and it starts to builds castles in the air. We individuals have monkey mind which jumps from thoughts to thoughts; like a monkey jumps from tree to tree. According to a popular saying, Excess of everything is bad. Hence we have to watch our thoughts as well, for the reason that off and on our thoughts lead us in an imaginable world that we forget what is up-to-the-minute around us. We become absent minded, loose our concentration and focus. Whenever this chain of thoughts gets settled in our mind and we are being along at a certain conclusion and that conclusion impacts on our behavior and attitude.

Resembling to above instance: when the baby elephant had a thought that he won't be able to free himself from that rope, this single thought will let other thoughts comes up such as I will be tied my whole life. I won't be able to move freely. My freedom is at the discretion of my master etc.

Let's assume you saw your dream car on road. A single glance at that car will be enough to stir up your imagination. You may jolt driving it in your mind, showing it to your friends and relatives, going out with your boyfriend/girlfriend on a long drive and what not.

In both of the above scenarios situations were unlike and so were the thoughts. Somehow our thoughts are also dependent on our current situation. The elephant was tied, so he was getting negative thoughts. In the second instance of seeing dream car, it twisted excitement, hence it attracted the fascinating thoughts, in fact a chain of fascinating thoughts.
Our belief system and thoughts has become a double edged sword impacting us a lot both in positive and negative ways. Many a times you will see someone smiling when they are alone or someone in tensed mode. At times you may observe someone physically present in front of you but is lost somewhere else. It's all the inclined of thinking.

THOUGHTS PROVOKE OUR EMOTIONS AND OUR BEHAVIORAL RESPONSES.

I DON'T BELIEVE IN TAKING RIGHT DECISIONS, I TAKE DECISIONS AND MAKE THEM RIGHT.

The above quote said by Ratan Tata reveals his belief system that once he takes a decision in his business he makes all efforts to implement it in a correct and positive way so as to achieve the desired results.

Similarly if we look at corporate world, in corporate world there is a hierarchy system which is charted. Let's say there are two diverse individuals heading two different departments. One believes that he can get the work carried out through commanding his juniors while other believes that he can get the work carried out through guiding his team. As both leaders are working to achieve their organizational goal however the approach of both of them would be different because of their belief system. Because that particular belief system will comes along two different thoughts between those two individuals. For that reason the attitude, feelings, action, habit and personality of both would be different.

The thought process of working professionals should provoke them to improve and to learn something new which can help in developing a new source of income, so that they are not dependent on their employers for their living. Only such thought process enables in emerging the new age entrepreneurs from salaried employees. As opposed to it if the belief system of employees enables them caught in the net of their comfort zone, down the line availability of cheap labor, tough competition and other factors can take their jobs off. Due to dynamic business environment and tough competition, economic conditions can get worse anytime. Be it employee or employer, no one is loyal to each other when it comes to business profits and cost cutting. Everyone in this world is trying to grind his/her own ace. The belief system which enables us to keep the rapid pace with dynamic environment, helps us to move forward in life.

Let's now apprehend it in context of past experience. If you had a bitter experience in past, Whenever you recall that past experience a pain would be felt in mind which will disturb the whole thought process, that indeed will act on your destiny. We have to take it into consideration that whatever behavior we are receiving from other people is only the final product of the above thought process cycle. This final product can be released not only through speaking; however it can be released through vibrations, behavior and actions.

IF YOU THINK YOU ARE A FAILURE YOU WILL FEEL LIKE A FAILURE. THEN YOU WILL ACT LIKE A FAILURE, WHICH EMPHASIZES YOUR BELIEF THAT YOU MUST BE A FAILURE.

ON THE CONTRARY, IF YOU THINK YOU ARE A WINNER YOU WILL FEEL LIKE A WINNER. THEN YOU

WILL ACT LIKE A WINNER, WHICH REINFORCES YOUR BELIEF THAT YOU MUST BE A WINNER.

Let's do an illustration. Hang on, let me share an experience. As I cited earlier our blooming brain need a toy nine times out of ten. One night at dinner time, I went to my father's room to serve him the dinner. When I entered his room, television was on however he was not watching the program on television. He was thinking something. From his looks, I could figure out that he was a bit tensed and obviously tired. Nevertheless, the point behind sharing this experience was the property/nature of our mind is to think and it will keep functioning every now and then. It's in our hand how we want to operate it.

Time for an illustration: Speak yourself this sentence five to ten times daily

- I am tired, you will feel tired
- I am worthless, you will feel useless and worthless
- This world is not for me you will feel like leaving this world and you will start living in isolation, and may get despair
- I hate my life you will feel like committing suicide

When you speak the above sentences you will observe a flow of negative energy in your body and mind. Why? For the reason that what you think your mind gets such programming signals and it behaves accordingly.

As opposed to above; in the morning speak to yourself:

I am fresh,

I am energetic ,

I am the best,

Success is convinced for me

Today is my day

By saying these things you will attract positive energy towards yourself, which will help you in making more correct and productive decision. You will less prone to make mistakes. You will twitch achieving results. Likewise I cited earlier that mind is like a child, so if a child who plays chess, he/she comes along with the intellectual capacity. If a child plays violent games somewhere down the line they will come along with a violent and aggressive nature. If a child plays problem solving riddles/puzzles he will mug up the problem solving skills. Similarly the type of thoughts mind gets, our mind will be directed in that direction. Our behavior, perception, attitude, feelings, action and personality would be an attractive one if our thought process is positive.

Opposed to it if we are influenced by a negative approach and negative thoughts our behavior, perception, attitude, feelings action and personality would be like such that no one would like to sit beside us, to talk with us.
Negative emotions exist only for the reason that we give them our consent to enter in our mind and then keep them alive. We feed them by continually thinking and talking about things that are negative.

The choice is ours whether we want to see ourselves in the first category of people or in the second category of people.

2. THE QUALITY OF YOUR THINKING DETERMINES THE QUALITY OF YOUR LIFE

"**QUALITY OF LIFE**" has quickly become a catch-all term.

What goes around comes around. If you think that you are a winner, you will walk out as a winner. However if you think that you are a looser then you will keep losing in every aspect of life. Once you build a perception (thought) about yourself, you are likely to keep an eye for evidence that justifies your perception and discount anything that runs contrary to it. Someone who comes along with the belief that he is a failure will view each mistake as its proof. When he does succeed at something, he will chalk it up to luck. Any milestones achieved will be considered as a fluke. That is why the quality of thinking matters a lot, because it determines the quality of our lives.

The quality of our thoughts determines the quality of our feelings, and based on those feelings we see ourselves as being good for something, or not that good. Our actions are the practical manifestations of our thoughts. For that reason if we think positive we will act positive and we will achieve positive results, which will make positive changes in our life and vice versa. It is quite clear, for that reason, we must bring about a change in the way we think in order to bring forth happiness and a sense of fulfillment in our life. A good thing about our brain is that it willingly adopts any changes that we bring about in our thinking patterns.

MY THOUGHTS MANIFEST MY REALITY. I MANIFEST MY DESTINY. SUCCESS IS CERTAIN FOR ME.

Remember? In our childhood days we erudite, Better alone than in a bad company; one rotten apple spoils the other fresh apples if it comes in contact with them. Similar is the case with people having negative thoughts. Those, who are influenced by negative thought, will come along the same attitude and they will be distracted and won't be able to capitalize on the available opportunities.

All of us have thousands of thoughts per day. The bottom line is that all these thoughts are energy that is shaping our world and every day of our life. It is out of the question to track each thought we have every day. The only way to track what we are thinking is to capture or remember the thoughts by paying attention the way they make us feel every day. If it is making us feel good in our mind, everything is fine however if it is creating a woe in mind we have to keep an eye around for another toy for our mind. Whenever we put out a low vibration thought for any situation, it turns out to be a curse. However whenever we bring forth a high vibration thought for any situation, it turns out to be a benediction.

Our thoughts create our words; our words create our world. To craft a better world for ourselves we have to implement a better and positive thought process in our life. A good thought is like a good quality seed which consists of the potential of becoming a fruitful tree. In order to improve possessions in life we have to mend our thinking.

The happiness of our life depends on the quality of our thoughts. The state of our body depends on the food we eat and the exercise we do. Similarly the state of our mind depends upon thoughts and emotions that take up in it. Thinking is a raw material for our brain. It's a food for our brain.

Every thought has its cause and it also has its effects. Let's consider a situation:

Situation: Weekend is just around the corner and a colleague asks in a group conversation what your plan is for weekend? Someone say: I'll watch movies, someone prefers frolicking online, and someone prefers attending seminars and reading books. Everyone has a different plan because they have different thought process. The one who thinks to spend time on weekend will sit online, will watch movies or play some games. The one who think to utilize the time and advance himself/herself will prefer reading books, attending workshops or seminars. Such thought will certainly pay off in the long run. It is your Thoughts that leads you in a direction where you understands the difference between spending the spare time and utilizing the spare time.

An individual who thinks that a toned up body looks attractive and builds confidence within, he will plan to join health club and will start work out and may be able to achieve good results. His life will certainly mend because he will start feeling fit. There is a thought in mind that as I have joined the Health Club, I will certainly improve my health. This thought will boost him morally. Now after joining the health club he will be involved in various types of workouts which will help in future and he will be able to get a good physical outlook. This achievement of being in shape was once a THOUGHT in mind. As opposed to it those who think that joining health club is threw away of time and money will never think to join and holding down to suffer obesity and other problems. For the reason that prior initiating any action there exist a thought behind that action. It can be related with any assignment of our lives.

Decrease the quantity of thoughts, surge the quality of thoughts. Thoughts can be your best friends or it can be a snake in the grass.

How to upturn the quality of thoughts:

Think Good

Think Productive

Think Positive

After completing their education (post-graduation) two friends apply in a company for jobs. They were shortlisted and called for an interview. They score well in all tests such as writing, online test, technical knowledge of their field, aptitude test. However in the last round one was rejected and the other was selected. The last round was one on one interaction with company's HR Head and with their department Head. They gave them a situation and ask them how would have they got on with such situation. The purpose of this scenario was to check the thought process of the candidates. As one candidate was selected and other was not for the reason that his thought process and approach was not considered feasible by the company's management. The quality of thinking was the reason for one's selection and other's rejection. In consequence it was that quality thinking through which the concerned was able to pull in his living and meet his expenses. He can for that reason also plans to increase the quality of his life henceforth by consuming the products and services he wishes to, by satisfying his needs and wants; for the reason that he has a source of income. And what was the primary reason for getting the job: Thought Process. Hence quality thought process is very crucial in determining the quality of your life.

Peace Pilgrim said "If you realized how powerful your thoughts are, you would never think a negative thought."

The thoughts we entertain are a key part of the process of creating the life we want. Our thoughts bring forth our emotions around the events and people in our lives. They are the impetus to action, and better actions lead to better results. And the reverse is also true. When we make judgments and focus on negative thoughts, we craft negative emotions, which lead to negative actions.

While keeping an eye at the above picture have you got any thought?

There is a famous story of a frog, who decided to climb a tree and reach to the top. This was just a thought he got. After getting this thought he started to climb the tree. Soon some others frogs piled up and started shouting that it's out of the question. However the frog that was climbing the tree makes it successfully and reached the top. He reached the top, for the reason that he was deaf and he was not listening to other's demoralizing words that it was impossible and he won't be able to make it. He was under an impression from other frog's actions and gestures as if they were motivating him. This thought provided him the confidence and he reached the top. Through this story we should hit the books that we all should avoid all the negative noise around us and we should think positively. Because,

The word impossible itself says I M POSSIBLE. **Audrey Hepburn**

Quality of thoughts is directly governed by the environment within which we are living. Our thoughts are directly influenced by what we see, hear, feel, taste and touch. Our thoughts form our belief which forms our values. We are the average of five people we spent most of the time with. It is for the reason our mind is influenced by our surroundings and the company we keep. Let's figure it out with an example: In Mahabharat; Duryodhan had a company of Shakuni, whereas Arjun had company of Lord Krishna. Duryodhan's thoughts were manipulated by Shakuni, who kept on provoking him all the time, whereas all Pandav's were guided by Lord Krishna. Similarly in case of Ramayana as well; Kekayi (Bharat's Mother) was in company with Manthra. Both of them (Duryodhan and Kekayi) were living in such an environment that their thought process was manipulated and rest the history we all know.

THOUGHTS CAN PUT OUTS WARS.

It happens often that whenever we have to make any critical decision we have to consider all the parameters, all the pros and cons, available resources, the risk and return associated with that certain decision which we are going to make or which we refrain to implement. To consider all such parameters we have to think logically, rationally and practically. These critical decisions can be related to opting of professional courses, deciding which career to opt for after completion of studies, choosing the better half; so on and so forth. These decisions are so critical and important that whole of our life depends on it. If such decisions seems fruitful our lives can turn out to be a heaven and on contrary it can turn out to be a living hell as well. That is why importance of thinking cannot be ignored. The quality of our thinking is primarily subject to the environment we are living in. Likewise a meritorious business environment helps a business towering heights similarly a healthy emotional and intellectual atmosphere helps in uplifting the quality of thinking.

The environment that influences our thoughts factor in the company we keep, our friend circle, and the people we are in touch with in daily routine. In fact the programs we watch on television also have an impact on our thoughts.

If we are continuously involved in watching hatred programs such as murder, crime, rape, extortion what makes us believe that there are good people as well, those also exists. Many a time a normal person becomes a criminal by getting the ideas from such programs for the reason that what we watch influences our brain and our thoughts. Our belief system starts operating in that negative direction.

Much of our mental ill-health followed up from our dysfunctional thinking. If we can recognize the power of thinking and set ourselves free from that power, we can help find our way back to well being, peace and joy. It is just one thought away. By understanding quality thinking better, we can help ourselves and others avoid the pain. Thinking is power and it is or duty to use this power for good. If we will think well, we will thrive towards doing good and we will achieve good. Because

QUALITY OF THINKING DETERMINES QUALITY OF OUR LIFE.

3. BEING OPTIMISTIC V/S BEING PESSIMISTIC

The pessimist sees difficulty in every opportunity. The optimist sees the opportunity in every difficulty. Winston Churchill

Optimist seek valuable lesson in every reversal or setback however pessimist sees excuses in every difficulty. The DIFFICULTY level and type is same, however for optimist there is an opportunity to grab and capitalize on contrary for pessimist there is an excuse for backing down. A pessimist will always find it like a hard nut to crack. At the end both will achieve different result. One will come through and other will face failure. One will be spoken highly of self and perhaps other will be criticized. Their life will be different, once this hard time is over. It is for the reason that the quality of analyzing and thinking has changed their life.

Good and positive thoughts are always spoken highly of and hailed; they bring prosperity. They have a solution oriented approach. As opposed to it bad and negative thoughts are for good considered as hostile. Everyone wants to be in a syndicate of such person, from whom there is something good to hit the books. Where your thoughts go, so does your attention. If your thoughts are rotten you are likely to feel stuck. Whatever we focus on, increases in our life; it is for the reason we attract that thing towards us.

A person who is thinking positive, he is coming over the chemistry of his/her body. 50% of the battle is won if we have won it in our mind by thinking that YES, I can do it.

The way we view the world can say a lot about our mental and physical well-being. It influences our decisions. Optimist believes in the beauty of the world and alludes towards optimism. They are future oriented who makes an effort to build a better over morrow. As opposed to it pessimist often chose to believe in the negative outcomes in life.

When we always focus on what could go wrong, then in that case any opportunity we gets we will be scared to use that opportunity thinking and believing if it's not gone our way. On the other hand optimistic people are their own best friend and self-motivator.

Pessimist people are the worst enemy of themselves.Pessimists are data driven; they never do anything that cannot be measured however optimistic are goal driven and ready to pay the price for success. Pessimists are small thinkers. They keep low expectations in life. It keeps them away from the life they desire. As opposed optimist are big thinkers. They keep high expectations in life as they believe in their potential and power.

We are not born with optimistic or pessimistic views. It is a cultured behavior through opinions of others, past experience, through the environment in which we are living and through the syndicate we keep. Our life is controlled by the programming carried out by our brain. The THOUGHT PROCESS of our brain is influenced by its programming and this programming is developed by our surroundings. Those great people in past have achieve greatness for the reason that of a different set of programming their brain did.

Nowadays (the time of competition), creative and critical thinking is admired and appreciated by everyone. It is for the reason our modern problems require modern solutions. Today everyone wants to achieve more in less time with less efforts. And for that, creativity and critical thinking is required. The interesting fact of our brain is that it is divided into two parts. One is conscious mind and the other one is subconscious mind. For creative thinking we have to use our conscious mind however our system is designed in such a way that 95% of our life is derived from our subconscious mind.

If we are optimistic, i.e. positive thinkers then only we can be creative. A person with a negative thought process cannot be creative. They are more likely to have the nature of crying more and giving less wool like a drop in the ocean.

Majorly, it is easier to become richer for a rich person. Why rich becomes more rich and poor stays poorer? It is because of the belief system. Poor people have the beliefs from the family that life is a struggle, it is like getting into hot water to become rich and they won't be able to make it to that level. These all beliefs get registered in our subconscious mind. Till the age of seven a child's brain is programmed and the future of that child depends on those programming. After seven it is the repetition only. That is why it is essential to come along with a positive thought process right from the childhood time. It becomes the duty of the parents. Later in this book there is a chapter in which, I have discussed parent's role in developing thought process.

Negative thoughts are not bad. Thoughts are valid being it positive or negative. Both compassionate a vital role in shaping us. Whenever we get a negative thought what we can do is: fall in with that negative emotion and process them in a healthy way. By processing it in a healthy way that negativity will blew away and we will be able to grab the opportunity from being got into hot water. But what if we are not able to conceive it in a healthier way; we have to change that thought. Let us understand it with the help of an example:

Stuck in a traffic jam and feeling irritated and popped off? The thought, "I can't stand traffic" will send signals from your brain to your body to speed up your breathing and tense your muscles. Whereas the thought, "I can't control this might make you feel unwind," it will send the signal to your body to calm down. Traffic jam is a situation where you just have to hold our horses to get it cleared so that you also can move forward towards right on the money. You will certainly get such thoughts that I might be late, my time is being thrown away. On the other hand by apprehending and processing these negative messages in a positive way i.e. traffic policemen are leaving no stone unturned to get it sorted for us and once it is cleared I will precede further, will impacts in a positive manner.

In general optimist achieve more, have better health and hold out longer than the pessimist while pessimist give up early, are prone to dejection and struggled a lot.

Positive thinking will let you do everything better than negative thinking will. Zig Ziglar

4. GLEAM OF HOPE

There is saying that 99% of people work for those 1% people who never thought to quit; because winners are not those, who never fail but those who never quit. They see opportunity every time, they get into hot water. So, doesn't matter how much your life becomes harder, how many times you got into hot water, just keep an eye on that one good reason that keeps you motivated to fight against the odds.

Life is like between a rock and a hard place and challenging and whenever you face setbacks after setbacks, problem after problem, it can get very hard to stay optimistic and keep this same perspective of resilience that is found at the macro level. It becomes really a challenge to remind yourself that you are strong and that you can get through whatever problem you are facing. When life is tough, giving up for good seems like the easiest option. On the road to destiny, every person will be tempted to give up midway.

In the course of this hard time if you keep your cool and calm and have a positive thought process, you will certainly find even a single reason of not quitting. That one reason is more than enough to keep your dreams alive and to keep you moving forward. Recall and keep in mind all those people who doubted you and said that you will be a failure forever. Don't quit because you have to prove them wrong. Don't sacrifice your lifelong legacy, greatness and pleasure; just for a temporary pain that you are getting right now.

In the middle of every difficulty there lies an opportunity. Albert Einstein

Most of us give up when we don't see our dreams turning into a reality. I know it's quite like getting into hot water and staying in the state of contentment when you got various problems in your life. Never give up; the beginning is the hardest nine times out of ten. You haven't tried everything yet so don't trigger any negativity in your veins.

In this journey towards success some turn around and go back other stay committed and move forward. What's interesting is both of them travel same distance; some opt to go back to where they started & others moves half way ahead and reach their right on the money. Giving up is the worst thing to do. You will be considered as losers & no one wants to be a loser. When we give up on our dreams, we die while being still alive. It's better to die trying than living like a dead.

On the way towards success some sparkle and some shatter, those who made it, they also know that they have got a hundred million reasons to walk away, however they just need one good reason to stay. If you have found that one reason, congratulations you have joined the 1% club.

There is no human being on this planet that goes through life feeling up 100% of all the time, feeling at seventh heaven all the time. All of us suffer setbacks, face failures, all get caught up in the things we should not and loose our way. Some of us remain lost forever while some of us find our way back to the path we were destined to travel. These are those 1% people who never quit. Whether you stay lost or find a path is a choice, whether you beat yourself down or lift yourself up is a choice. Whenever we are given options to choose, we always thinks what is better for us and then execute. Similarly a person with positive and right on the money (goal) oriented thought process will choose and will find the one good reason for not quitting, while the one with negative thought process will find million reasons for quitting. Change your thoughts and you will change your life. Whenever you are lost ask yourself some questions to come to light the valid reason

Write down your reason WHY? WHY must you succeed; why must you get healthy; why you must achieve whatever you decided for yourself? WHO are you doing it for? Why must you keep fighting?

There is a reason and when you find that reason it will light up a fire in you and everything you do. It will wake you up early and keep you awake late. Will inspire motivate you to push harder every time. It will enforce you to try a different way or to find a way in achieving your goals and will not let you to ever give up.

You will have low moments, but you will never stay there. Life is short; you only get one shot at this human experience. Under the sun you stressing about will not matter at the end, problems were there, are there and will be there. Let it go. Focus on the thing you love and tail your passion. Be grateful of this life and the time you left and make the most of it. Once your mind start thinking in such a way you will certainly come to light a reason or a motive that will fill up you with life and energy. I will be at seventh heaven once everything is perfect. Nothing will be perfect. Every time a new challenge would be knocking at the door till the time it is not come apart into. Don't hold your horses to get everything perfect. Be happy and everything will get perfect. Once you feel happy and positive then you leave no stone unturned to overcome all the obstacles that you face heading towards perfectionism.

Feed your mind with positive and powerful thoughts. Positive and powerful thoughts bring forth wonders. Start reading books and have a mentor. It really helps. Science has proved that physical exercise can lower despair, narrow down the stress and release endorphins from brain which is considered as exultant hormones. That is why it is equally important to keep our body as fit as our mind, we want to. Because according to a famous proverb a sound mind lives in a sound body. When we will feel physically fit then our mind will also feel fit. It is for the reason that from our own belief our mind gets vibrations of being fit. As the proverb says; a sound mind lives in a sound body. It bear out that physical fitness and mental fitness are in consensus to each other.

Whenever we are ill or tired or not feeling well, during that time our mind is also not able to function properly. So it also becomes a responsibility that if we wants our thoughts to be healthier we should also make efforts to keep our whole body health. Go for a gym or some running. Start a physical workout and you will see humongous change in yourself. You will build a confidence and this confidence will entail you to improve attention, focus and your thinking ability. Stop holding yourself back locking into the prison of your past. It is these past experiences, which impacts our belief system. If these past experiences were not good try not to recall them. People with positive approach mug up from their past, work hard in their present and improve their future while people with negative approach just stay with their bitter past experiences and eradicates their present and future. Try to keep yourself involved in the work that excites you or motivates you.

You will never allow a thief to come in your home and hold out there rent free, so why allowing a thought to make away with your joy by entering inside your mind. If you have been robbed once, after that you will make all the efforts to keep yourself aware and alert so as to avoid yourself being robbed again. Similarly we have to make all the efforts for not letting a bad thought striking our mind and if it does trail up to our mind, eradicate it by some other positive thought. If not, try some exercise, any game that you like and you will get rid of that negative thought.

In the course of that tough time recall your goal and start focusing on how to achieve those goals. By implementing such practices you will cut out those million reasons which are keeping you down and keep progressing ahead.

The success is sweet however the secret is sweat. Life does not go as we plan. You will face lots of censure, you will lose friends, you will lose your credibility and more worsen off and on you will lose your identity and even doubt your existence. Just recall that one reason that provokes you not to give up and that reminds you why you have to be successful. It is written in Bhagwat Gita: You are not week, your time is. This time too shall pass and it will pass. Think positive and march forward for your goals. Mug up to let go and learn to pass over. Someone did wrong to you, let it go. Moving on letting go is best revenge.

Those who are successful, who are living an amazing life are not lucky they move on quickly. They let go all negative and focus on positives. They don't seek sympathy from others because they had a bitter past experience. These people don't cheat on their future with their past. They stay committed to future, for the reason that their future will suffer if they don't let go their past.

Moving on is the one reason. Just think of that one good reason that keep you alive, awake and motivated and move on.
It's a piece of cake to blame those that have victimized us. If they didn't do this, I would be where I want to be; if it wasn't for them, I'd have more money. Most of the people get so caught up in blaming that they hold down to blame their whole life and also when the person is gone from their life, because blaming is easier than moving on.

Ask yourself: When you let go all the negatives and keep moving on. Who wins? Who succeeds? Who bring forth the best life? It's you.

The primary cause of unhappiness is never the situation but your THOUGHTS about it. Ekhart Tolle

Worried about an upcoming presentation? The worried thought, "This will be awful, I am so anxious" ,will went off you feeling panicked and on edge, whereas the thought, "I am doing my best, that's all I can do" will help to send signals to your body that it's okay to be calm and unwind. An individual who lose his temper in such a situation and gets panic might not be able to give a proper presentation and he or his company may suffer. However the one who thought to do his best and focused himself/herself will be able to outperform his competitors. In consequence it is rightly said by Ekhart Tolle that," The primary cause of unhappiness is never the situation but your THOUGHTS about it."

5. COMING ALONG WITH A POSITIVE THOUGHT PROCESS

There is a law in psychology that if you form a picture in your mind of what you would like to be, and you keep **and hold that picture there long enough, you will soon become exactly as you have been thinking. - William James**

Positive thinking is not about expecting the best to come about every time however going for that whatever comes out is the best for this moment. Our every thought is a consecration; let us shower ourselves consecrations and energies by thinking positive. For the reason that, we never speak to anyone more that we speak to ourselves in our head. As a result it becomes our duty to become kind to ourselves by thinking positive.

Dream lofty dreams, and as you dream, so shall you become. Your vision is the promise of you shall at last unveil. – John Ruskin

Whether the glass is half empty of half full? Optimist will say the glass is half full, while the pessimist says that the glass is half empty. The purpose of this experiment is to reveal the two different prospective of analyzing a similar situation. Person with negative prospective may fell like getting into hot water in a tough situation however, the person with positive prospective may observe the forthcoming opportunity. In fact the emptiness in glass is another opportunity to refill it again.

According to William Shakespeare-**There is nothing either good or bad, but thinking makes it so.**

Positive thinking transforms and enhances our life. There is a saying: **AS IS THE GRAIN, SO IS THE MIND.** Source of energy for our body is good and balanced diet, similarly source of energy for our mind is a good thoughts. Likewise for a healthy body we need a healthy diet, for healthy thought we need a healthy emotional diet, i.e. information that we read, hear, observe or watch. This information becomes a part of our life.

Like food like mind. Not only it's what the physical food we are eating impacting us, in fact the vibration behind it also impacts our mind and health.

In a slaughter house where there are lots of birds and animals are kept. Whenever these species will see the other one getting murdered it will ripen a fear in their mind. All of them are kept in cage or tied. Those animals will cultivate a thought of hatred and fear towards the person who is selling them for profits. Whenever we eat such food, what are we eating? We are inputting the vibrations behind that food. These vibrations are fear, screaming, anger, aggression.

If we are feeling thirsty we will have water to quench our thirst. What we think and observe?

- Whether the water is clean?
- Whether the glass is clean?

However we never think whether the vibrations are clean or not?

In our childhood we were taught to pray to God and thank God prior having our food. There is a strong reason behind it. It makes the vibrations in that food clean. Children not only eat, what their mother or grandmother cooks, they also input the vibrations behind cooking that food. Hence we all should keep this thing in mind that while cooking we will not focus on our challenges and problems, so as to make the environment positive.

Keep in mind that you have to be self-reliant for this you have to be self-sufficient. Make the body healthy, strengthen the life force and raise the morale high.

Don't let the mind be discouraged, but elevate yourself by focusing the mind on the higher because the mind is your friend as well as your foe. This is a famous verse from Bhagwad Gita (Hindu's Mythology) and its message is: amazing man should elevate himself with his own help. Do not let yourself fall down, because you are your own friend and your own enemy too.

Let's fathom it with the help of a couple of instances:

- Television is an imperative and integral part of our lives. We watch it on a daily basis. There are lots of options available for us; we have to decide what we want to watch. If we make a habit of watching crime shows, it will cultivate a feeling in ourselves that humanity doesn't exist. If we watch good and healthy motivational, philanthropist programs, our minds programming will be carried out accordingly. What will make you believe there are good people when you watch murder, jealous and criminal sort of programs.
- In a charitable organization, or at a religious place you will always come to light with philanthropist people doing good deeds such as distributing foods, clothes to the needy, worshiping God, spreading awareness and motivating people to help the needy. Whosoever remains in such environment will always try to do good deeds without seeking any reward against it.
- Music and songs; Muttering songs, listening to music or songs act on our mood. Listening to motivational songs impacts in a totally different manner as listening to a sad or bleak song. It's a piece of cake to listen to motivational songs when we are successful or at seventh heaven, however if we encounter failure or if we are feeling down we like sad songs. In fact in such scenario we should also try to listen to energetic and motivational song

so that we should not get negative thought in our mind.

We can change our way of thinking by changing the inputs of our operating system. This is the emotional diet of our brain which is fed to it daily. Likewise good nutrition food provides energy to our body; similarly good emotional diet provides energy to our brain. Our emotional diet should be of high energy. These are positive vibrations, meditation, atmosphere of our homes and offices, getting involved in productive things, maintaining a solution oriented approach instead of problem oriented approach. A lot of time, we tend to focus on our unpleasant past experiences, which cannot be changed. Due to this the situation becomes ever worse and our negative emotions takes over by recalling the bad past experiences. Consequently, we have to learn to move on towards our future by concentrating on our present.

There are some exercises that may help in coming along with the positive thoughts in our mind. Right emotional diet in beginning of day, such as meditation, recalling, thanking and praying to almighty God will come along with some positive vibes. Counting on you and quoting yourself, if I am being fair and square then nothing wrong can come about. On the other hand if we are like a man of straw, we will be surrounded by negativity nine times out of ten. A man of straw considers others the same as himself and never trust anyone.

Allow your mind to continue free float while thinking about the ample possibilities. Dream big and define an ideal vision for yourself and blow yourself towards achieving your goals by becoming blue- sky thinkers. Just do good deed with pure on purpose and try to pull in consecrations by those good deeds. Law of energy says what we think; comes up, for the reason that we are radiating it with our thoughts. If we fear our mind will catch it, if we have faith on ourselves our mind will catch it. In both scenarios it will function in two different ways. When right emotional diet will be observed by our mind then we will be radiating rationality and optimism. It's our choice.

Things that can really help and attract us towards positiveness:

- Spending more time by doing things that we love: Whenever we do something that we love and enjoy, we enter into dynamism where time flies and everything else melts away. We enter into a world where we forget everything and keep concentrating on that vary thing which we are doing. This also helps us in concentrating and focusing.

- Sharing thanking notes: Sharing written thanking notes really helps us focusing towards optimism. While writing thank you notes to someone who has been grateful to us, our minds kept reciting and recalling the good experiences that we had with that concerned individual. It releases those exultant hormones in our body which also attracts optimism.

- Reading good books really helps in coming along with a noble character and our thought process.

- Construct the thought what your life should be, do not bring forth the thought what is it right now.

- Learn to forgive yourself and all those whosoever is there in your past that is to be forgiven.

- If indulge in an argument or conflict, we should make sure to sort it prior drift off. By doing this we will be eliminating the negativity continuity for the forthcoming days. Taking a minute or a pause for two minutes after every hour really helps in creating a right thought to get back to work.

- Praying and thanking God for anything and everything that we have; comes along an element of satisfaction in us.

- Spirituality and meditation attracts us towards optimism and keeps us away from greed, curse, hatred and violence. A person who stays away from such negative emotions matures a strong and a positive attitude.

- Before going to bed in night, the last thought and memories should at all times have to be positive It is for the reason that our subconscious minds also works while having forty winks and if we feed our mind with buoyancy while sleeping the next day we feel energetic and we come along with a problem solving attitude through this exercise.

To come along with a positive THOUGHT PROCESS, think and analyse about all those people who are successful as per your perception. When you focus on success you become solution oriented, future oriented and goal oriented. Once goals are identified and we focus on accomplishing of our goals we try to find out solution to all of our problems and this enables us towards a solution oriented approach. Through these approaches we can achieve all of ours goals and dreams. It is the quality of Optimism that helps us in making The Impossible, Possible. Optimist seeks the good aspects and the lesson to be learned from any setback.

Illustration: In your whole life you might have encountered such scenarios in which you were leaving no stone unturned to figure out a solution to your personal or professional query, or trying to emerge from a problematic situation throughout the day, however you turned down the day reaching nowhere. However when you woke up the next day morning your mind has got the answer/solution to that situation. This is because of our subconscious mind. Consequently it is precise significant that prior sleeping we should go to bed with a positive mindset, because our subconscious mind works 24*7 and never rests. Therefore it becomes our duty to take care of our subconscious, by developing a positive and rational THOUGHT PROCESS.

-

I EXIST SO I THINK. I THINK SO I EXIST.

6. OVERCOMING FROM A NEGATIVE THOUGHT PROCESS

Human brain is capable of accomplishing great things, provided we should have clarity to think dream and create. We are all responsible for sending ourselves negative messages and unless we make efforts to change direction of our thoughts those negative messages will start dominating us and will bring forth chaos in our life. Almost forty to fifty thousand thoughts pass through our brain in a day. We have to be clear about which thought is required and which to be tossed.

It is said that "Destroying a week is easy than destroying a strong."

Be it a week situation, a week opponent in business, a competitor in game or a thought. A thought is weakest when it is charted up for the very first time in our mind. If we feel like it is a negative thought that is distracting us, we have to cut it short then and there. It can be carried out by thinking something positive, replacing that thought with the other positive thought. Or try to pursue your hobby, playing a game you like, singing a song you like, by doing so our mind will be distracted from that negative thought. Changing the sacraments, habits of children is easy. It is easy to mold children the way their parents want why? Old habits die hard or die in no case, for that reason whatever habits or sacraments are developed in the initial phrase of a child life it becomes a part of his life. It's like a habit for that child.

Similarly thought is like a child, in the initial phrase when it strikes the mind. Then it keeps on evolving and manipulating our mind. If you feel like it is not good just kill it with another good thought and don't let that thought dominate in your mind and rescind it then and there.

Whenever a child bits his nails, or sucks his thumb the family members make efforts to hold back the child doing such thing. It is for the reason that in childhood those negative actions can be improved however if they are not tried to improve at that stage it becomes a habit for life long. It's never too late; however we have to correct it whenever that negative habit, action or the thought is weakest. If efforts are not made to correct the mistake in the initial phrase then later on it will become an attitude which will attract criticism. Later on that censure becomes a habit which is hard to change and mind has to hit the books a different way to interpret. In that case we have to guide our mind by writing. More efforts and time is required at that stage to change the thought which has turned a habit now.

According to a Russian Philosopher Peter Ouspensky there are four sources of negative emotions. These are

Justification

Identification

Inward Considering

Blame

Scenario: Alisha and Ayesha were close friends. Both kicked off their career together at the same post. However Alisha outperformed Ayesha and got promotion. Ayesha mind got a negative thought as both started journey from same place at the same time however Alisha is much successful than Ayesha. In such situation it becomes duty of Ayesha to think rationally that there might be some parameters which has caused this difference. By doing so, that negative thought will be abolished. However if she did not do so, this petty thought may raise a feeling of jealousy, ill will and may brought about a rift in friendship of both girls. Rectifying negative thought at beginning stage is necessary to avoid the possible consequences.

We are living in such a society where negativity is common, normal and natural. Off and on thought is bent from the other side, other person as well.

A negative thought can came along if someone

- Does something wrong to us, which we didn't like
- Abuses us
- Criticize us
- Litter around our surroundings
- Speak ill off to us
- So on and so forth

The thought of what others will think, has assassinated the entrepreneur in you. The thought what others will think refrains us from thinking out of the box and achieving great results. However the fact is that nobody thinks about you in the least. To get over from such situation we have to be responsible and accountable for our thoughts. By taking responsibility and accountability we ripen a nature in ourselves that we should not bother our emotional health because of some other person actions, habits or deeds.

The more you try to forget the unpleasant past experience, negative emotions, regrets and fear; the more you recall it. So forgetting is not the solution. Then what?

Running away is also not a solution because; all of those negative or positive thoughts are connected to our memory. The past experiences through which we are getting negative thoughts were a part of our memory.

It seemed that most doomed people are held back by some event that occurred in the past that they cannot let go of. They are still stuck in their past and THE IF'S AND BUT'S of those past experiences. To change your thinking and change your life, you must make a decision to get over them and to get on with your life, no matter what came about. Till you remain a slave to the past, which cannot be changed in any case; you will find it like getting into hot water to move on in life. We have two options to choose from:

Either to focus on what has happened in the past

Or to focus on future possibilities

THE OPINIONS OF OTHERS:

It's our life and we have the full right on our life. Let us not give others the opportunity to run and control our life. Many a time it ensues when someone says something to us, whether it is bad or good, whether it is offensive or polite; our mind keep reciting it and we swirl in the swamp of thinking and our mind jolts asking endless and pointless questions, which makes us falls in the trap of negativity. So it becomes our duty of not allowing any other person to control and manipulate our thoughts and mind.

Our thoughts and feelings are not dependent on other people and situations. These are dependent only on me. Try to conserve energy in situations that are not favorable. I cannot change their behavior; they will hold down to do the same in future. I can't change them. What I think is in my control. My life does not depend on how they behave with me. Bless those as well who are not nice to us. Don't give others the power to cut short your positivism and your energy. **Try to avoid arguments**.

Thought is just an energy. For that reason we have to be very careful about what we think. Thinking positive will bring forth a positive energy. Create one positive thought daily and you will be blessed with a positive energy. On the other hand if a negative thought is twisted you will suffer from negative energy. Negative energy attracts negative behavior and negative emotions. Hence whenever you encounter a negative thought, promise yourself of rescinding it then and there. Don't let yourself dancing on the tunes of negativity.

Our mind is like water. When water is put in a jar, it takes the shape of that jar. When it is put in a glass it takes the shape of a glass, similar is the case with bucket and pot. Likewise, our mind is also similar to water. Whatever thoughts we will put in it will lead us towards that type of attitude and personality.

In the process of overcoming from a negative thought our environment can help a lot. Be vigilant of what environment you are having around yourself. Whenever we visit to any peaceful and religious place like temple, then the environment of that temple influences our thoughts, similarly if we will keep holding out in a negative environment then that negative environment will also impact us. We have to teach our mind what is to fall in with and what is to ignore.

A chaotic mind practices a chaotic life. If we keep on reciting any negative thought, that negativity becomes a part of our personality. If we are good we will come to light good in others and the vice versa is also applicable. As a result, it becomes our responsibility to think good, look for good and observe good, for the reason that whatever we think about other people becomes a part of our personality.

To overcome from this negative thought process try to find and keep an eye on one quality in each one whom you get in touch with, it is going to be about me not about them, for the reason that I have started placing positive energy in myself by keeping an eye on and observing the positive energy they have. By doing this I am attracting my mind towards positivism. I have a choice what to grab from my surroundings or my world, what I absorb is what I become.

Keeping an eye at weakness or coming to lights about faults in others is a piece of cake and keeping it in mind is easiest. Then it is natural to hold on to it for very long. Then we kick off believing it. Faults or negativity of others which distract us or acts as an obstacle in our progress; keep in mind: it's their perception, their nature, their attitude or their mood right now. It's not about me it's about them. They are not hurting me by such attitude, they are just upset.

A thought which immediately shifts me from disturbance to stability is the need of the hour. Earlier a thought was put out that brought about a pain now we have to bring forth a thought that will heal.

Whenever we get hurt by any negative emotions our mind kicks off churning as:

I can never forget

I don't want to forget

Why should I forget?

Because of this churning we are not able to heal ourselves from the negativity. Now is the time that we should ask question from ourselves:

- Should I take you (negative thought) seriously?
- What's one good thing about this situation?
- What's one thing I can do differently the next time to have a better outcome just around the corner?

What's one thing I can pick up from this?

Once you start asking such questions the negative thoughts will not be able to dominate you and you will be attracted towards optimism. What other people thinks or believes is none of my business. It's a piece of cake to fall into negative thoughts when you think about what people may say or think if you do or do not do something and may trap yourself in analysis paralysis. Getting stuck in your head and in thoughts like these will drag you further away from your goals.

We are living in such a society where success is always appreciated and a failure is looked as a culprit. However it is the failure which that teaches us, not the success. It is the failure that molds us in developing our risk appetite, our character and helps us in improvisation. Failures are the turning point, that can turn stone into a diamond. We always learns from our failures not from our success. A failure who tries, who improvises and innovates is far better than the one who never fails because he never give it a try.

We all are trying to prove ourselves in front of others. Whenever we start living on other people's expectation, we are killing ourselves from within. Whenever we encounter failure we are afraid of facing the society. These can be our neighbors, relatives, friends and all who are our known. On the other hand whenever we succeed we are not shy to flaunt of it in front of all those.

You don't have to prove anything to anybody. The competition is not with the outer world. It is you competing with you only. Most of us keep on considering what the other people, the so called society will say. We start living and fulfilling the expectations of people around us. Most of the time we feel like or think:

What our society will say?

How they will behave on my actions?

How our relatives or friends will react?

These thoughts distract us in achieving our objectives. However, the truth is that people don't have that much time, attention or energy to think or talk about what you do. Way to get over from any thought you feel like is not required (negative) is to:

QUESTIONING THAT THOUGHT

Whenever a negative thought knocks on the shoulder and tries to flinch growing in mind simply questioning that thought.

Should I take you seriously?

Most often you will get the reply as: no. Generally whenever we are tired, hungry, overburdened or focusing on our awful past experiences negativity can bash to cloud our mind.

Ask and evaluate yourself about the top sources of negativity in your life? It could be lifestyle, people, websites, environment, music and anything. Then attempt to find what can be through to spend less time or to change these sources.

Spending time with more positive sources and people, working towards improving in lifestyle, engaging self in some hobbies such as playing favorite game, reading the book you like, cooking etc. can really help us and keeps us away from negativity. It leads us to forget the past and focusing on present. The primary cause of unhappiness is not the situation but how we consider it and react to it. Mostly irrelevant and unnecessary things bother us a lot. **Stop making mountains out of molehills and the mind will be more controlled and focused.**

Deep breathing really helps. Take a minute pause, close your eyes and take deep breaths for 3-4 minutes. When we control our breathing, we also control our thoughts.

Take a halt, have a sip of water. Going for a walk, running or any physical exercise helps our mind getting out from unwanted thoughts. Be grateful for a few of the things you may often take for granted. When we get negative it's like a child play to forget the positive things our lives. We start playing ducks and drakes with our positive and memorable experiences that we had. Keep in mind if we have a roof over our head, if we are having meals three times a day, if we have family and friends and clean water to drink we are blessed. Thank that almighty for all what you have. This practice keeps us away from outside noise and makes ourselves more stable.

Self-discipline begins with the mastery of your thoughts. If you don't control what you think, you can't control what you do. Napolean Hill

Simple ways to get to a positive kick off is to wake up early. Because when you wake up early in the morning when approximately 80 to 90% of the people are sleeping, i.e. around 4 am or 4:30 am, you get a confidence that you are ahead of those who are in bed right now. As you are awake you have more time comparative to others. Early morning is the time which can be used in productive works. Early stage entrepreneurs can use this time in making their business plans, making the strategy for their business growth. Students can use this time in studying. By waking up early you get the time for exercise, you have time to read books. It will motivate you from within. So start waking up early, with a positive note and see the difference.

If you have not control your thoughts through your feelings, you have no control of your LIFE. If you do not control your life, there is someone out there that has no issues in controlling it for you, to manipulate you in every way possible and make you believe what they want you to believe. Take control of your thoughts in order to take control of your life.

"Real wisdom is avoiding all thoughts that weaken you." Wayne Dyer

7. DIFFERENCE OF OPINION

"The vibration you need to match it to reality you want and you cannot help but get that reality." Albert Einstein

You cannot hold back it from coming about, so bring forth the vibration of reality we want. Whatever we really want from our life we have to craft vibrations like that only. It can be carried out by our thinking. Whenever we think about achieving anything we start taking actions which are required in its achievement.

Thoughts have the ability to bring forth new relations and friends. There are ample students in a class, in a college lecture and there are so many individuals working in an organization or in our locality. Yet we have only some special people whom we consider as our friends. The reason behind it is same thought process. Whenever two people think alike, they start enjoying each other's company. They start liking each other and a bond is established between them. Whenever two or more person have different views or beliefs, or a consent is absent on any niche it attracts discussion or a debate. It can be in office, at an event, social pile up and in family. Human beings hold out in such a society where they keep on interacting with each other. Whenever two or more individuals have discussions it is just around the corner that somehow they will have different opinions. This difference exists because of our different ways of understanding, interpreting and conveying. Similarly in family, it is our thought that makes this bond strong.

Family is a blend of senior citizen, adults and children. It is obvious that each and every family member will have different prospective to comprehend different situations, because of a different thought process. Family conflict comes along when members of a family have different beliefs or viewpoints, when family members misconstrue each other, when someone gets his/her feelings hurt and develops resentment, and when miscommunication leads to mistaken assumptions and subsequent arguments. We Indians at no time are taught to talk to our parents as adults and that is a big problem.

Many a times it has been observed that teenage children and their views are not taken seriously by their parents, which has serious implications in future. Whenever there is a discussion between parents and their children it brings a feeling of being small and incompatible in teenage child. It can also be accompanied by feeling of guilt, regret, defeat. Similar is the case with adult child of that home.

Feelings like my parents turn a deaf ear to me; my way of doing is not good; they never consider my opinions and thoughts; they will turn a deaf ear and if they will listen they will not be brought around. It came along a sense of being powerless and forces the young adult/child to think that he will do it his way. This is the time when they come at hiding the things from parents, they jolt lying and manipulating.

Not even for teenage children it also comes up with the grown adult children in the house. It is the duty of the parents to figure out the mindset and thought process of children. They have to give respect to their children's view as well. There is a perception in our society's mind which makes them ignoring the thoughts and suggestions of their juniors and children. Initially it doesn't bother however slowly and gradually it ripens a feeling of guilt, being passed over, feeling of being small in that individual whose point of view is snubbed. Because of these scenarios children these days are more becoming more violent and stubborn.

Similar is the case with newly married couples and young adults. After marriage there is an addition of a new member to the family. Hence it becomes really imperative to respect and consider the views of that new member.

The time has changed so fast and dramatically. Today's era is the era of innovation, implementation of new ideas, modern thinking? The young generation gets comfortable and get used to it easily. However the elder generation feels like getting into hot water to implement new ideas and thinking. Today is the time where people want to enjoy their wealth, improve standard of living, living life to the fullest. As oppose to it our previous generations including our parents and grandparents they were of the mindset that getting meal for the day is more than enough. They don't want to upgrade themselves. This difference of opinion between one generation and other generation regarding values, lifestyle, and beliefs attacks below the belt and disturbs the whole family. It is for the reason that our parents and grandparents keeps on reciting those old rituals and habits which we believe is outdated and should be replaced with the current trend. This is what we call it as, "Breakup with Parents."

Off and on young child or teenager wants something out of their life and parents don't come to an agreement and child has to curb the desire to see parents at seventh heaven.

What child wants if it is not in concurrence with society or parents choices, there is a price to pay? With married couples the situation turns even worse when they feel like getting into hot water to adjust for the reason that of different thought process of spouse and a different thought process of parents in laws. It is human psychology among individuals to think that they are right at everything they do. Due to this belief each and every individual tries to proves and justifies, more worsen later on the conversation turned into an argument.

This is one of the biggest reasons of increasing in divorce cases today's era? Because either it's all wet between husband wife or it's all wet with in laws. If it is with parents the young couples feel like that they should be living alone and far from parents? If it is with spouse it may lead to divorce. Difference of opinion will be there nine times out of ten for the reason that all of us have our own priorities, needs and desires. However it becomes the need of the hour to figure out each other, respect other person's views. It is applicable for every relation.

Let us understand with the help of an example:

When we were kids we used to share everything with our parents. If parents don't ask us then also we used to tell them about how our day went, what experiences we got etc. However when they grow up as a teenager or young adult they start hiding things. Now are underway of manipulating and lying to our parents.

It comes up with most of us. The reason for this is

Because, initially during childhood parents used to listen to their children, they fall in with their opinions, emotions and acknowledge their children.

A few years down the line child had bunked his school for a movie. He went to the movie with his school friends, later that day he shared this experience with his parents, however that day he felt rejection from his parents. It's obvious as bunking school and going for outing is not good. However, it was the atmosphere around that child which made him think and decide that he should go for movie, because his friends are also going. This atmosphere made him think like that. As his decision was not appreciated by his parents and he was scolded that day. This has moreover flourished several other thought in his mind. The experience that he had in movie hall with friends, that past experience with friends which made him feel good will program his mind in a certain way and the past experience of getting scolded or beaten by parents will program his mind the other way. If all are doing it in group or friend circle I should also do. The company of his friends, he is associated with has provoked him to do so. It is for the reason that his thoughts which were influenced by that atmosphere.

The other time whenever the group will think for any such activity, child will get two types of thoughts. One, he will recall his past experience of enjoyment he had the first time he went for movie with his friends and the other that he encountered with his parents. These thoughts when converted to actions will either letup him to go out with friends or will provoke him to go out and hide this experience from parents, so as to avoid parents scolding.

Now the parents think that child has discontinued doing that thing however he has stopped sharing the things with parents. It is because of the two different environments, two different past experiences and two different belief system; the thoughts of two different individuals are different.

Children and teenagers are prone to be on thin ice of evolving other bad habits such as smoking, drinking, eve teasing etc. For the reason that if they see others (friends and colleagues) doing it, it will enforce their thoughts as well. It is the duty of parents to guide the child by interacting with him and by counseling his mind that whatever he thinks is right, for the reason that he is living in such an environment. However that thing is not right for him, such as bunking with friends, smoking and drinking. It brings respect mutually.

If on the other side, the other way is opted such as scolding, beating or threatening. Then there are consequences.

This is the reason there are councilors in school for children. Imagine a child is talking to stranger, sharing his views with a stranger rather with his parents. Why?

The councilor will consider his mistake as a mistake, which was considered as a sin by parents. Because councilor won't have any critical or judgmental thought in his mind. On the other hand if child tells it to his parents then he gets other type of vibrations. This feeling and thought cultivates stronger as the time proceeds. A child who obeys to his parents 50% of the time gets vibrations that he doesn't obey to parents. 50% of the time he obeys 50% he doesn't. However parent believe that child does not obey, the same thought gets surrounded in all home among parent, grandparent, child and even in neighbor and relatives. This energy and thought provides a message to child that he is like that only. Then later in future child will become like that only. Later on the problem may be worse, when the child will become a teenager and adult. To avoid such consequences, parents should understand that the child is having a different opinion, different environment and a totally different thought process.

It is a type of emotional abuse. Unlike physical abuse, being emotionally abused doesn't leave you with visible scars that can be like a child play to detect. Emotional abuse weakens the individual's emotional development and sense of self-worth. It can have lifelong damaging effect. Emotional abuse is the biggest reason of despair. In healthy families, parents help their kids move out and hold out their own life. Toxic parents on no occasion want to let their children go however they always point out that the house, the money, and the food belongs to them. They want their obedient children to stay by their side. For such parents, child's private life and personal space not exists. Life becomes a challenge, when young child tries to help his old and helpless parents. In particular in that old age there is an element of eccentricity and noxiousness. Toxic parents don't understand the way child guides them and they continue to blame that child does not help them however how much they have helped him in his childhood.

Every child is on thin ice of suffering in this world full of imperfect adults and childhood scars cut deep shaping our entire lives. Parenting is for good a reflection of one's best self and worsts self. Creating a vibration that child is not obedient, child is stubborn will make child that only. Research shows that for children of any age; parenting that is warm, sensitive, and supportive provides a great chance of child developing strong academics abilities, good social skills. It's the quality of relationship between parent and child matters however what if the quality of relationship is absent. That is why parents need to be educated about how to discipline and communicate with their child without damaging that relationship. There is a requirement of parent training program. Through such program this difference of opinion can be cut out. As a parent we should understand that this is not that child now however he has become an adult. Many adult and young teenagers lost contact with their parents for the reason that they didn't reach agreement to their children's opinions. As we grow old our needs change however our parents hold down to see the same child they saw in earlier days, so the young adult feel like that they are encroaching in his/her freedom.

On the other hand parents feel that the child is not respecting them which bring forth misunderstanding and an element fading to let go. By changing our thought process we can change all of our morbid habits. If a child is always tensed and afraid of his parent's mood, it makes the child emotionally week. This may leads to more problems henceforth in future.

For toxic parents, an emotional set about is synonymous with love and attention. In such families, kids know how to come to light what mood their parents are in by the sound of dropped keys or by the scrape of footsteps. Such children hold out in constant fear and apprehension. These types of toxic parents often get offended if their kind actions are treated with suspicion. They claim that they have gone through everything for their children and yet their children are ungrateful.

Child life:

A child when enters this world, he is dependent on his parents for all his needs, he contemplates himself helpless and needs the attention. Whenever someone asserts authority on child he feels helpless and inferior. He may feel inferior when some other child gets a higher grade in class. Most of the time children learn from their parents. Child's future personality and his behavior are totally dependent on the parents. If he sees his parents betraying, lying, manipulating and dominating on spouse he will be disturbed emotionally and will pick up such things that will impact his personality and behavior. He may come along with a feeling of hatred. Parents have to be very careful of what they are talking, how they are behaving. If a child sees his father dominating all the time and his mother is helpless, his thoughts will become like; all males dominate which will enforce him to dominate as well in future. However if he experience a good co-ordination between his father and mother his thinking will be like that by co-coordinating with each other a successful home life can be hold out. Parent's behavior impacts child's thoughts.

School teenager: Teenage is an extremely critical phrase of life. In the course of this span they are not a child and want to take their own decisions. Whenever parents show confidence in a teenager child the child feels confident. However if the parents feel that child is wrong and discuss it, child aspects at it as a boring lecture. During this time child go through some hormones changes. Teenagers hate whenever there is a negative discussion being done about their friends. It makes a teenage child feel like that he is not capable enough to choose his friends and teenagers kick off to draw distance from their parents. They can get caught by ill will or inferiority complex due to multiple reasons. Parents have to respect the thought process of their teenage child and a suitable co-ordination is a must. Let us ponder a situation below

Avnish was going through his teenage phrase. All of his classmates, college students and other group of students of his age used to travel to tuitions and school on their bicycles or motorbike. However, Avnish has not picked up yet, how to ride a bicycle or a motorbike. Due to which he has faced a lot of taunt and criticism due to which he has become a victim of child abuse and inferiority complex most of the time. He became irritable and kicked off losing interest in studies and other activities, because of this complex. His parents didn't guide him and trained him as they were afraid, he might meet with an accident while driving. Due to such mindset of his parents and such rational thought process led Avnish to be a victim of ill will, inferiority complex. Instead of having rational thought process, his parents should have opted a practical and positive thinking approach.

Teenagers feel good when parents ask for his opinion. It made them feel prestigious; however on the other hand if parents think that he should not be involved in discussion just for the reason that he is younger, he may think and feel the other way. They think they are not kids now however on the other hand parents keep their eyes at them as a kid, then there comes along a conflict between them.

Not even with teenagers, young adults are equally influenced by the negativity of the environment. In our country we are living in an environment which is mostly dominated by male member of the family. As the teenage child has grown and has become an adult, now the real problem flinches. Now we have two male adults member in the family with a generation gap. Their belief system and thought process is different.

Likewise there is a breakup and divorce in the couples; moreover it also comes up with the parents. The reason is the same, the thinking and belief system differs. That brought about the differences.

It is our societies mindset and thought process that all parents wants their child to flourish, to grow, to outperform and have all the happiness that he or she wants from his life. It is just around the corner getting into hot water and unimaginable for our society to see or observe such scenario where the adult children hold backs all contract with their parents and break up with them. Nobody makes choice to breakup with their parents overnight; it's that they were living in a morbid family for such a long time. This was the THOUGHT PROCESS of parents that led child to break up with them.

Let us ponder certain scenarios. **These below experience are eye opener:**

- **Not apologizing even when you are wrong:** Just for the reason that I am your parent or I am senior to you, I cannot be wrong. I won't apologies.

- **Blaming or finding fault for good**:Not backing up the child in his own decisions, and if any of child's decision proves to be wrong they kick off frolicking blame games. However if it founds to be a good decision they by no means back down from taking credits.

- **Manipulating**: They twist the truth and manipulate things in such a way that only justifies their opinion.

- **Overreacting and unpredictable**: They overreact on small things and their behavior is unpredictable.

- **Mocking**: They mock you, point out your shortcomings and bring up the things which are sensitive to you. However if they are wrong you are not supposed to utter a word.

- **Expectation:** Expecting the adult child to deal with adult problems but still making him realize that he has no rights in assisting you, as you being his parent don't need his suggestions or opinions. Expecting the child to trail parents instructions however if he fails later then the culprit is child only. On the other hand if he come through then taking credits for his success.

Apart from some scenarios discussed above there are other so many situations which enforce children to breakup with their parents and stay away with them. The above discussed scenario clearly point towards the type of thought process such toxic parents usually have. They always think that their behavior will refine their children. Moreover it attacks below the belt and impacts the other way round. In such families a child believes and considers himself as a culprit. Later the children will get dragged to adult scandals. All such experiences leads to serious emotional issues such as eating disorders in children, sleeping issues, feeling insecure all the time and when parents again complain about the behavior of child of eating disorder, irritability, sleeping issues then it adds salt on the burn.

Expecting child to improve himself however pass over his future plans, the belief that my child should keep an eye on my instructions, however if he/she fails then blame is on child. Such type of thinking of toxic parents make the child believes that there is no private and personal space for the child.

"The mind is its own place, and in itself, can make a heaven of hell, a hell of heaven." John Milton

8. EMPATHETIC THOUGHT PROCESS

A coin consists of two facets. Our prospect and way of keeping an eye at things decides our actions and thoughts. Organizing our thoughts helps us in developing the skill of empathically thinking. This type of thinking enables us to think from the other person's prospective. Empathy helps us in breaking the ice and establishing a good relationship. For one person it is a numeric six while for the other person it may be number nine. We all are living in our own sort of reality however it is vital for us that we should try to understand and experience other's reality. This can be done by empathy, i.e. thinking and analyzing from other person's prospective.

The reality version in which we are living is the only thing which we know and it is limited by our senses and experiences. Relations can only be prevented when we takes into consideration the other person's prospective as well. Empathically thinking enables us to uphold a harmony between our relations. It can be any personal relation as well as professional relation. Presence of empathy between relations builds a strong bond. It is for the reason that of this empathy we can understand even without saying.

It is essential in every relation. A couple who understands each other and has empathy in their relations their married life is far better than the one who lacks empathy. Similarly empathy element is moreover required in parent's children relationship, in business between the customers and the businessman. Empathized thought process demands to put you in the shoes of the other person and analyzing the situation from his perspective as well. It is a quality through which a businessman can come through in business by analyzing and reading the mindset of his consumers.

What a consumer wants?

How does he feel?

How his taste and preference changes according to change in fashion, change in season or how consumer responds to change in trend?

Similarly if a teacher can understand the behavior and mindset of students, he can design the curriculum in a way that suits student's learning.

All those entrepreneurs who are struggling to make their venture a big business; consider for a minute that it might not be your lack of talent or lack of skills that are holding you back. Instead, it is your beliefs and thoughts that keep you away from giving your best. It is for the reason that what we think we start believing.

Creating a more positive atmosphere can lead to outstanding transformation. It does not get at that positive thoughts have magical powers. But optimistic thoughts lead to productive behavior, which surges your chances of a successful outcome. The only individual who can think positively is the one who has implemented a positive thought process in his/her life. Positive thinking along with empathy can do miracles.

Empathetic thought process can help us in understanding other people's opinion without asking them directly. It is an inherent quality which can be developed. Empathetic thought process can help and prevent someone from committing suicide; it can prevent someone from going into depression and other can keeps us away from other negative consequences.

Most of the time, a general discussion gets converted into an argument. This happens for the reason, whenever we indulge ourselves in a discussion with someone; having a different approach, a different Thought Process and lack of empathy.

To understand the challenges and problems of someone, we have to put ourselves in their shoes. We should impose the quality of empathy. There is no purpose of discussion with someone who lacks empathy. Those concerned will always get a discussion turned into an argument. It has been observed in most of the orthodox families, as the time proceeds there arises differences between parents and children, sometimes between husband and wife. Empathetic Thought Process helps us in overcoming those differences. Our mind articulates a map that leads us to whom we are today and who we want to be in future. The goals that we want to achieve for ourselves, we can learn to grant those wishes by evolving our empathy. No one is competent enough to do everything on their own; we all are dependent on our relationships, society and friends. Therefore it becomes equally significant to think from other person's prospective as well. Without empathy even a genie cannot make us reach the seventh heaven.

Empathy is seeing with the eyes of another, listening with the ears of another and feeling with the heart of another."

You don't need a better phone, you don't need a better home, and you don't need better circumstances. You need a better mindset. Thoughts determine what you desire, action determine what you get. Being true to self is one of the smartest choices we make in the course of our lifetime. You should always keep an eye for means to please yourself and only then to please those around you, and this is not about being selfish, but rather about knowing yourself and being true to your own needs and desires. If you aren't blissful, how can you expect to make others feel like at seventh heaven? You can't give others something you don't have for yourself. Through Emphatic thought process we can get peace, harmony, progress in our personal as well as professional life. Be it a positive or negative, our thoughts are very powerful and they mold our lives. In consequence, it is vital that we should recognize our thoughts.

Henry Ford said, "Whether you think you can or cannot, you're right." In other words, what you think is what you get. That is why it is critical that you know your thoughts.

9. PARENT'S ROLE IN DEVELOPING POSITIVE THOUGHT PROCESS

According to **Law of Attraction** positive or negative thoughts bring positive or negative experiences into a person's life. It doesn't matter whether hurtful words are intended to bring about pain or not they can leave mark and memories from a short time to lifetime. The remarks are followed up from our loved ones, such as parents. Many studies have shown that parents who have a negative approach will have children with a higher susceptibility to depression. During childhood and teenage phrase, children are dependents on their parents; parents have a major role in composition of coming along a strong emotional connect.

Our coming generations will learn by observing us. Hence it becomes our duty to nurture them in a correct form. This can only be done by developing a positive and logical thought process. As discussed earlier, that our thoughts are directly linked with our emotional diet, Parents can put in by following ways:

Some Do's and Don'ts---

- **Show me some respect, for the reason that I am older:**

It is certainly vital for people to give respect where it is due however there are limits. The thought that being older I deserve respect from all those who are junior to me is irrelevant. It sends a message that once you got to a certain age its ok to behave in a disreputable or unethical manner because other people should respect you no matter what.

Therefore, if parents are elder and toxic, being commanded to respect such behavior just for the reason that they are older is confusing. That is why one should not come along with such belief system. The thought should be, Give respect and take respect whether someone is junior or senior, inferior or superior.

It is the law of nature that all existing individual will go through their adolescence, teenage phrase, young adult and old age phrases. Hence, believing in the notion that if someone is elder to us in age is more knowledgeable, more smart, more intelligent is completely unjustifiable. As a result not all advice from old people are supposed to be listen or acknowledged for the reason that foolish people grow old too.

- **Disciplining the Child in Front of Others**

At times, parents lose their patience and scold, yell or even hit their child in front of others. This will seriously impact child's confidence, and the feeling of shame arising from this method of discipline will be hard to shake off. This emotional support can only be developed when all the members of a family understands each other. Empathy plays a crucial role. In such type of situations the one who has empathized thought process will get on with the situation more positively.

- **Empty Promises**

Promising your child for something but not fulfilling it later. It comes apart the child's trust and make child feel betrayed. It's a way to teach a child not to trust anyone. By making empty promises to our children they will moreover learn the same and will develop a belief that this world is not trustworthy and selfish. And when someone progresses with such thought that all are selfish and cannot be trusted, this thought will impact our feelings, attitude, action and personality totally in a different way, which isolates the concerned from the society.

- **Avoid Unhealthy comparisons**

Ghoulish comparison leads to feel jealousy and resentment among siblings or friends. You by no means speak highly of your child for his/her achievements and do not show pride in hard work. Sarcastic questions and remarks like why you walk like that, why you eat like or selfish wishes such as," that may make the child feel that there is something wrong. Using offensive words such as you are too short or fat or skinny

Signs of emotional abuse from parents

- Offensive words such as ugly, too fat, short or skinny – degrading child based on their appearances; Selfish wishes such as I wish you were different child or comparing with the other one of his/her age.
- You will never make it or you are a looser
- Criticizing on a skill that children haven't learned

In most of the typical families such scenarios are common; however we should apprehend the criticality of it. It directly impacts the entire thought process cycle of the victim. All such things bring forth negative vibrations and negative thoughts. It cut short child's independent needs and desires leaving the feeling unworthy of anything other than following parent's whims. Child feels like burden and they unconsciously hide their needs, and problems to avoid wrath of parents. Making a child feel like burden, by making him think that it is costing too much money on his education and in his upbringing. It makes child feel that they should not exist in this world or they don't deserve to be alive. They diminish whole sense of identity of child.

Parents are supposed to be the one you can depend on unfortunately many parents say emotionally harmful things that can have a negative and long lasting psychological effect. Majority of the parents focus on what child was unable to accomplish rather than what he has achieved. And their reactions and remarks hurt their child's emotional health.

During teenage child's preferences and taste changes. They come at some new hairstyles, they are obsessed to join gym, making new friends, they are attracted towards contrary gender and they are passionate about a part time job along with their college. It is the parents of the child, whom the child shares some of these thoughts. However it is very sad that in the course of that phrase child faces rejection and criticism most of the time. Nothing is more embarrassing than being harassed by own parents. Such experience make the child feel that if his own parents humiliates him, then what will come about when he jolts interacting with the outer world. No one has the right to shame anyone for his/her likes, dislikes, physical appearance. From a toddler's height to a teen's work ethic to an adult child's marriage, a range of studies shows that moms and dads may be among the worst judges of their kids. But there are deeply adaptive reasons for parents' enduring misconceptions.

Parents should show confidence in their young adult or teenage child. Typically in Indian middle class families its been observed that whenever a teenage child or a young adult shows his willingness to do his own business, he is not supported by his/her parents. The support first should come from family, however it is not alike that.

Important point to note here is whenever a new business is started first of all a stranger who becomes our first customer trust us and make us realize that the business has potential of growth, as opposed to it the near and dear ones always criticize and are always involved in plugging holes. Instead of finding flaws and focusing on negativity family has to come forward to support on the positive aspects.

Critical thinking and questioning can help the child and parents getting out of this.

10. SCIENCE BEHIND OUR THOUGHT PROCESS

Our mind is like machinery (operating system) which is operated by the thoughts we feed in our mind. These thoughts serve as programs which controls our life.

Science has revealed that brain is designed to download program for first seven years of a child life by observing people, around age seven consciousness kicks in and this consciousness use those downloaded programs to bring forth behavior in relationships, family community etc. Our mind is divided into two parts conscious and subconscious. Conscious is a habitual mind which makes us to do our daily tasks properly however the subconscious mind is creative and is put through to personal identity, spirituality.

Thought is an inside job of our mind. We get various thoughts from our wishes and desires i.e. subconscious however we are operating from habits, i.e. our conscious.

Our life which we are living is already controlled from downloaded programs

The conscious mind is a creative mind however the subconscious mind is a programmed mind, a habit mind. Our conscious mind orders and our subconscious shadow it. The intuitive (conscious) mind is a sacred gift and the rational (sub conscious) mind is a faithful servant. Those who listen to their conscious mind, they are the one who do something out of the league. They generates employment, they generate ideas, it is these people who creates history. We are living in such a society that honors the servant and has forgotten the gift. This thought process has become a habit and an attitude of our society. This thought process has led us to believe in herd mentality and has kept us away from thinking out of the box.

People may hate you for being different and not living by society's standards, but deep down they wish they had the courage to do the same. Kevin Hart

Flowing with the flow of the river is easier than standing in the river against its flow. The one who dare's to go against the flow has the real courage. This is the zone which provokes us to think out of the box. This is the zone where the real skills are tested and where leaders are born. For mounting a creative thought process we have to get involved our conscious mind actively. Tim Ferris said, "If you want to win the day, you have to win the morning, however in reality to win the morning you first have to win the evening". Our evening routine is as powerful as our morning routine. Because our conscious mind works 24/7, therefore planning the next day before going to bed alerts our conscious mind. And this mind makes us an early bird to execute our day the way we planned. Have you ever observed: many a times whenever we have to do some important task the next day, we get up early without alarm. Occasionally when we are working on an assignment and stuck somewhere, the other day when we wake up we come to light a solution. This all comes about because of conscious mind which was working while being asleep.

Reviewing our goals every night before sleeping really helps in achieving them for the reason that these goals gets registered in conscious mind which works 24/7. By programming our conscious mind we will be programming our life. Almost 95% of our life is the result of programming of our lives done by our mind. Our thought programs our mind and our lives.

"Whatever we plant in our subconscious mind and nourish with repetition and emotion will one day become a reality"-Earl Nightingale

11. SENSE OF SELF-IMPROVEMENT

Our mind is like machinery (operating system) which is operated by the thoughts we feed in our mind. These thoughts serve as programs which controls our life.

Science has revealed that brain is designed to download program for first seven years of a child life by observing people, around age seven consciousness kicks in and this consciousness use those downloaded programs to bring forth behavior in relationships, family community etc. Our mind is divided into two parts conscious and subconscious. Conscious is a habitual mind which makes us to do our daily tasks properly however the subconscious mind is creative and is put through to personal identity, spirituality.

Thought is an inside job of our mind. We get various thoughts from our wishes and desires i.e. subconscious however we are operating from habits, i.e. our conscious.

Our life which we are living is already controlled from downloaded programs

The conscious mind is a creative mind however the subconscious mind is a programmed mind, a habit mind. Our conscious mind orders and our subconscious shadow it. The intuitive (conscious) mind is a sacred gift and the rational (sub conscious) mind is a faithful servant. Those who listen to their conscious mind, they are the one who do something out of the league. They generates employment, they generate ideas, it is these people who creates history. We are living in such a society that honors the servant and has forgotten the gift. This thought process has become a habit and an attitude of our society. This thought process has led us to believe in herd mentality and has kept us away from thinking out of the box.

People may hate you for being different and not living by society's standards, but deep down they wish they had the courage to do the same. Kevin Hart

Flowing with the flow of the river is easier than standing in the river against its flow. The one who dare's to go against the flow has the real courage. This is the zone which provokes us to think out of the box. This is the zone where the real skills are tested and where leaders are born. For mounting a creative thought process we have to get involved our conscious mind actively. Tim Ferris said, "If you want to win the day, you have to win the morning, however in reality to win the morning you first have to win the evening". Our evening routine is as powerful as our morning routine. Because our conscious mind works 24/7, therefore planning the next day before going to bed alerts our conscious mind. And this mind makes us an early bird to execute our day the way we planned. Have you ever observed: many a times whenever we have to do some important task the next day, we get up early without alarm. Occasionally when we are working on an assignment and stuck somewhere, the other day when we wake up we come to light a solution. This all comes about because of conscious mind which was working while being asleep.

Reviewing our goals every night before sleeping really helps in achieving them for the reason that these goals gets registered in conscious mind which works 24/7. By programming our conscious mind we will be programming our life. Almost 95% of our life is the result of programming of our lives done by our mind. Our thought programs our mind and our lives.

"Whatever we plant in our subconscious mind and nourish with repetition and emotion will one day become a reality"-Earl Nightingale